Typewriting
to Heaven...and Back

Karen Kaplan

Dear Dad,

You are not going to belive this but my
typewriter let me know it was time X' to
talk to you and that you were open and
waiting

Dad it's a 1940 Royal, like you use to take in
at the pawnshop, Wow

So here I go......

Karen

Yup tapping seems to be trans
mitting your thoughts and feeling
s to me.

Wow, a 1940 Royal

Who would o f tho ught it

Could connect

It must surely mean you and I

are open to the possibility of

transmission

Typewriting to Heaven...and Back

Conversations with my dad on death, afterlife and living

by Karen Kaplan

Offerings Publishing, 2020
ISBN: 978-0-9993135-2-7

Book design by Gilman Design, Larkspur, CA

Cover, vintage typewriter photo by Mirko Popadic, Shutterstock
Title page photo, Karen Kaplan
Back cover photo, author's archives

Contents

Preface

Dear Mr. Royal Typewriter,

How is it that I believe you called out to me, to tap to my dad? Are you aware of something I am not? Have your parts absorbed the energy of those who have moved in and out of our lives?

Perhaps you found yourself in a pawnshop, in San Francisco, absorbing the energy of Mr. Mac, a name customers gave my father, who founded the pawnshop and worked in it until his ninety years were over. Or is it that I resonate with you?

Is it my energy you have absorbed and my sadness and wonder that calls out to you? Is it my longing to have a conversation with my dad that motivated you to call back to me? I am baffled that I hear your call.

Death, dying, afterlife, heaven, spirit, soul, reincarnation, living the best life I can, meditation, inner piece, friendship, sharing life, love, health and non-attachment have been my questioning thoughts.

These thoughts were on my mind and heart the day I turned sixty, March 7, 2011. Now it is 2019, and I am sharing what happened to me. Who could have imagined I'd be tapping questions on a 1940 Royal typewriter and receiving answers on a 1960 Smith Corona? I wonder if those answers I seek will come as I type to my dad.

I begin tapping.

Introduction

HOW DID IT COME TO PASS that I would have conversations with my father nearly twenty years after his death?

It all started when I viewed the film, *California Typewriter*, at the Rafael Theater in San Rafael, California. The film stirred up strong emotions. Its message resonated; writers are rediscovering the power of the typewriter by using them to write the lyrics to their songs and the words in their novels.

I was on a mission to locate a typewriter. There was an odd and compelling voice in my head saying, "Find one, write on one and see what materializes." I wasn't sure what I would write but I was inspired to find a typewriter.

I searched antique markets. I asked my brother, who was running the pawnshop, to be on the alert for one. But none of these attempts brought that typewriter into my life.

Then it happened. I was enjoying my chai latte at Peet's Coffee in Novato, discussing that very film with my friends Liz and John. Liz said, very matter-of-factly, "I have an old typewriter that I'd be happy to give you." She invited me to follow them home after we had finished our morning drinks.

When we arrived, Liz opened the garage door and went inside. She grabbed a stool to help us reach the typewriter, but she was unable to climb up there. So I reached up and pulled down John's 1940 Royal. Liz said there was a second typewriter just to the right and I could take that one too. Now I had two of them. Interesting.

Next a voice in my head said, "Prepare the old shed for writing." I converted a dark and dingy wooden shed to a light, airy and safe place to write. I hired a contractor to install new floors of washed gray wooden boards and new walls of white wooden panels.

I placed a beautiful circular carpet from India in the center of the room, and found two interesting metal light fixtures and had them installed in the ceiling.

The inner voice now said, "Go out and find a suitable table and chair," so I drove to Petaluma, strolled Kentucky Street and found the perfect set in an antique store. I secured them in my Volkswagen Beetle Convertible for the short ride back home. I smiled.

Three weeks later, the typewriters were set up in my special shed, serviced, and ready to be tapped on.

I must now share with you something personal. Ever since the death of my father, I had been on a search to understand life after death, and to reconnect to the unconditional love my father gave to me in life.

Somehow, I just knew those typewriters and my search set the rest in motion for conversations with my dad.

That inner voice said, "Get out there and connect to those type-writers." So, I did. I sat at the perfect table in the perfect space. I felt this energy in my fingers. The words flowed easily. Questions, as well. I am not really sure where a few of those questions came from. But once they were out, they made sense.

My father's words flowed back, just as fast, as if he had been waiting all this time for me to ask. I felt a sense of relief as each answer came. I wasn't lonely when I typed. A few hours later I had filled dozens of small stationary cards: first with my words and then my fathers'. I felt so many emotions: sadness, love, wonder and laughter.

Each session at the typewriters began with that voice saying, "Get out in that shed. Put your fingers on the keys and see what happens." Then the energy in my fingers would calm down when

4

I pulled back the typing bar, inserted a card, centered it for tapping and the conversations resumed.

Maybe each of us is secretly seeking to understand death and also heal our hearts. Perhaps both can be accomplished through conversations with those who have loved us. When I lost my mother and then my father, I began reading books about death and dying written by those who helped the grieving heal. I recall one author suggesting that writing to a loved one and letting that person know how you were feeling or simply how your day went could fill the loss and ease the grief.

Perhaps that is why the Royal Typewriter called out to me, "Just write to him."

So, come with me as I tap on the keys of my Royal Typewriter and learn from the answers my father typed back to me on the Smith Corona Typewriter. I promise there will be moments that resonate with you, stir up laughter inside, maybe even elicit a tear or two, and possibly those moments will help you open to developing your own connection with a loved one.

Then, the next time you find yourself strolling through a garage sale, an antique store or a flea market, you may just hear, "Just write to me," coming from an old typewriter.

. . .

The Questions Begin

Dear Dad,

You are not going to believe this but my typewriter let me know it was time to talk to you and that you were open.

Dad, it's a 1940 Royal Typewriter, like you use to take in at the pawnshop.

So, get ready to hear my words.

First, forgive my tapping, my misaligned letters, faintly inked words, missed punctuation and spacing errors.

Seems to be part of getting use to the energy transmission between heaven and earth, you and me.

Dad, this film I viewed explored the re-immersion of writers using typewriters, rather than computers to write their novels, and singers, using typewriters to write their lyrics. They wanted to truly slow down and feel the connection to their words once again. The film fascinated me and moved me to find a typewriter.

Honey

It's all okay.

Remember my writing wasn't so legible either. I am sure your brother is still trying to decipher some of those old pawn tickets and sales tags I wrote.

Karen, your tapping seems to be transmitting your thoughts and feelings to me just fine.

Wow, a 1940 Royal. Who would have thought it could connect us.

It must surely mean you and I are open to the possibility of transmission.

Honey,

It is good to feel your connection.

I know you miss me.

I feel your sadness at times and see those tears rolling down your eyes as you drive in your black Volkswagen Beetle traveling highways 101, 280, 92 and once again 101 from Novato to Redwood City to work.

I know those songs you listen to stir memories.

I am always with you, safe within your heart.

I feel you too, Karen.

Dad,

Miss you every day. Your love was unconditional.

You made things seem possible.

You made ideas seem possible.

You gave me my name.

You said mom meant well.

Honey,

Of course, I loved you unconditionally. You were my daughter.

I was determined to name you.

Your mom meant well and I told you so.

She was just a little less capable and aware of how to show you.

She loved you unconditionally in her way.

I know it didn't seem that way at times.

But believe me it was.

MY DAD ALWAYS WORKED. He worked six days a week, to provide my mother, brother and me with a comfortable life. He got up at 6 a.m. and he got home just after 6 p.m. in the evening. He was proud of the business he had built. The pawnshop provided our family with many luxuries, others did not have. I felt that I was a very privileged child, able to live in a nice home, go to summer camp, travel and not worry about college loans. My dad was a calming force for me. He balanced out the sometimes-critical nature of my mom. While he wasn't overly affectionate, he always listened and he always wanted to know if I was okay or if I needed anything. He believed in me. We greeted each other with a kiss and departed from each other with a kiss. I always knew he wanted me to be happy and I knew he would be there to support me.

My mom had some wonderful qualities. She was organized. She was able to create a welcoming home for family, friends and all my college friends. She could put together a dinner for eight to ten guests with limited notice and with whatever was in the refrigerator or cabinets at the time. She held the highest position in the Eastern Star, the Matron position, and had the ability to memorize pages of rituals and deliver them in an eloquent manner. She could make 500 cheese blintzes in no time at all and prepared our yearly Thanksgiving Dinner for our entire family. She introduced me to the theater and exposed me to the Europe she found interesting. But Mom had very high standards for me. If I obtained a B grade in a subject, it should have been an A and if I received that A, she expected it. We never agreed on the type of clothing I should wear. She definitely had a set idea for the types of men I should marry and if they were not rich, or a doctor, or an attorney, they didn't meet the criteria. Mom found it hard to express her feelings. I had to tease her into telling me she loved me. "Of course I do," she would say.

• • •

8

Death and Other Questions

Dad,

Shall I tell you all the life that has happened since you left, or have you been observing it?

Karen,

The typewriter has connected us. So, continue your tapping to me. I'd like to hear your version.

Dad,

When I arrived at your house on December 1st, two hospice women sat motionless on the bench seat at the top of the stairs.

They said you had lifted up your arms towards the ceiling and then you were gone.

I screamed. I couldn't believe you were gone.

Dad, was someone reaching back to you?

Honey,

I am glad you screamed. I was in transition so it didn't bother me. You knew death was near.

I am sorry we did not say good-bye formally.

I did tell you to allow another man in your life the night before.

Hint, hint.

We are all helped to transition, by a breath exhaled, a reach or perhaps sleep.

Dad,

We were in route to you the day you passed.
Had you wished Darryl and I were there when you moved on?

Karen,

Each person has a different need when moving on.

You were there the night before. I know you and your brother loved me.

Please do not be so hard on yourself and if your brother is feeling badly, please tell him the same.

What matters is that we made many memories while I was there with you.

Know that we all do the best we can.

We cannot predict the end exactly, so we must live each moment.

We were all living each moment that day.

MY DAD WOULD HAVE NEVER MADE us feel guilty in any way. He would never have wanted us to have regrets. He always wished for my brother and me to lead happy lives. He was angry when either of us could have been mistreated by anyone. He was angered by the way my ex-husband was so greedy when settling our divorce. He couldn't understand how anyone could be so unkind as to take away someone's childhood dream.

. . .

Dad,

The night before you passed, you said for me to let a man in my life again.

Did you know you were leaving the next day?

Letting someone in, is challenging.

I tried Table for Six, J-Date and that E-Harmony site. The process is so unnatural to me.

But I will remain open in the future.

Dad, what are the important characteristics of that someone I should let in?

Karen,

I had a sense that time was getting closer, yes.

You know I only wished for a simple smile each morning from your mom.

A companion is important.

Someone who enjoys eating out, traveling and watching a good movie or TV show is a good thing.

Find that someone who provides you space to be you.

Find someone engaged with life.

A person who values family is particularly important.

Let someone in. Let someone in to care about you.

Share some happy times.

I mourned your mom as expected. Then I opened my life to companionship.

I enjoyed companionship the rest of my life.

I was lucky.

MY DAD FULFILLED THE PROMISE that he made to my mom at the altar. I tried. But on the day that my father told me he wished my mom would just get up with a smile on her face, I knew I could not stay in my marriage. I told my dad I was alone in my marriage. I told him I would rather be truly alone, than feel alone and actually be with someone. The affairs were more than I could bear. Dad told me to get the toughest attorney. He advised, "Don't be possessed by your possessions."

. . .

Dad,

It occurred to me that I never thought about how devastating it must have been for you to lose mom and then a few weeks later lose your sister.

I only just thought about it when I almost lost Darryl this past December.

How did you manage to seem so calm and move forward after so much loss?

I was trembling when I heard my brother was shot. All I could think was, I don't want his life with me to be over.

I don't even remember driving from Novato, over the Golden Gate Bridge, to San Francisco to see if he was alive.

I am so sorry Dad, for not thinking about your feelings of a double loss.

Karen,

You had just lost your mother. I had you helping me out at the house. I had you helping with funeral arrangements. You had to go through your mom's things and help me move her items on.

How could you have any room to understand Ruth's passing on me?

You also worked, had three sons to take care of and you lived one hundred miles away.

Karen,

I took one day at a time. I followed the year of mourning and then knew I needed to live.

That is why I moved the old furniture out to create space for a new chapter.

Please don't dwell in the past. No blame. Make now count.

I think your experience recently of nearly losing your brother

13

provides you with another lesson on loss.

Use it wisely.

Remember to tell your sons you love them.

Connect with them and let them know you are thinking of them.

Celebrate birthdays, invite everyone.

Connect with your brother regularly it will let him know he is important in your life.

Send people a thank you.

Don't let family get too far away. Keep in contact in some way.

Treat yourself. You work hard.

When life doesn't show up as you thought, be sad or be disappointed, do what you have to do to move through it. Then live your life.

MY BROTHER AND I touch base every Wednesday. We call this hump day. We connect to find out something good that might be happening in our lives. Since the shooting event in the pawnshop, I also try and see him at the pawnshop and bring him a special treat, just to let him know I am thinking of him. I connect weekly with my three adult sons. I also remember to connect with them before they take off on any trip and let them know I love them. All three, now, do the same when it comes to traveling anywhere. We celebrate the holidays together and of course Mother's Day. I let them know I am always there to listen and advise, when asked.

My father taught me to say thank you. He taught me to help others believe in themselves. He showed me how to support.

• • •

Dad,

Do you remember this event?

One of Suzie's twin sons, Gerald, was identified with Aplastic Anemia as you were living your last few weeks.

Treatment was at UC Medical Hospital on Parnassus Street in San Francisco, near the panhandle of the park. Remember, where Dr. Epstein's office was?

Dad, did you know that I offered Suzie the use of your home so that Gerald could live close by the hospital with his family during treatment?

Your home gave everyone a loving place to be together before Gerald transitioned like you.

Gerald was able to sit in comfort in your soft recliner in the TV room.

Sue and Ross could relax knowing he was comfortable in between treatments.

Everyone had space to sleep and Sue could cook in the kitchen. You had everything she could possibly need.

Honey,

Family was always precious in my life. You know that.

It is so good to know our home provided space for Gerald and his family during this intense time in their lives.

You made the right decision.

MY FATHER WOULD HAVE been devastated to think a young person like Gerald would pass away before he would. He would have done anything to help his niece. I know I did the right thing.

．　．　．

Dad,

Chrissy and Peter lost their daughter, Annie, in a fatal car accident, soon after your passing.

The loss was devastating, like the loss of Gerald for Suzi and Ross and their son Zack and his sister, Ashley.

Dad, did they find you?

Karen,

When a young life comes to a quick and unexpected end, there are no words of comfort, only listening and holding.

I was ready when I left.

I lived a well-lived life.

If the spirit world sees that it is my journey to connect with Gerald or Annie, then it will be.

Dad,

I remember your gratitude for each additional year of life you were given after your seven-by-pass surgery.

You passed on one of your received birthday cards to your cardiologist and Dr. Mackler, thanking them for another year of life.

You taught me that it is so important to show gratitude and to thank people.

This is a trait I practice in my life.

Thank you.

Karen,

I wasn't ready to die.

I had more life to live.

I focused on getting well.

I wasn't finished working, being with family and friends.

I was grateful to all those doctors who had the skills to give me more time.

I gladly sent those cards.

Honey, take care of yourself.

Find capable doctors who support wellness.

Keep your mind alert.

Read, travel, connect with others, work and enjoy family.

Dad,

I will.

MY DAD WAS WISE in a quiet manner. He was grateful. He showed his gratitude. Today, I find myself lighting my incense candle on my altar each morning and thinking about what and who I am grateful for about my preceding day. Today, all of the mindful practices suggest we start each day or end each day with one or more things we are grateful for. My dad was ahead of the mindfulness movement.

• • •

Dad,

Today I woke up once again thinking about your words the night before you left.

You advised me to allow another man into my life.

You were grateful to be admired and intimate after mom's passing.

I continue to be open to the possibility.

Karen,

Please be open.

We are not meant to be alone all the time.

Find someone to share a walk, a dinner, a cruise, and family and intimacy.

SINCE MY DAD'S PASSING, I have engaged in working, service, developing friendships, traveling and writing. But I am still reminded by his words, we are not meant to be alone. I am opening to the possibility. I am ready for all those activities.

. . .

Dad,

You never spoke about GOD, religion, death or your beliefs in an afterlife.

I didn't ask.

I wish I had.

Karen,

You are right.

We didn't have those conversations.

I don't know why not.

We went to Temple.

We celebrated the High Holidays with family.

We honored the dead at the cemetery, Jewish style.

I wore my Kiput and Talis in temple and at grave sites.

We stood under the Hoopa for weddings.

If I had known your interest, I would have shared with you.

So, make sure you have those conversations with your sons.

Tell them your beliefs.

No regrets.

MY FATHER SEEMED TO follow the customs that his parents followed and he was comfortable with. He had me attend Sunday school where I also learned the customs. We lit the candles at Hanukah, mom made latkes and I got a present, just because oil burned for eight days a long time ago. We didn't discuss the deeper meanings, which was something I was supposed to get out of Sunday school. I also thought it was odd that we exchanged presents on Christmas but I could not have a Christmas tree.

I am not at all afraid of discussing spiritual beliefs with my sons. They have laughed at my crystals hanging in the windows, wondered about the need to have the toilet bowl cover closed on the toilet, smiled at my smudging at all solstice times and inquired about my meditating, yoga and Qigong. They have enjoyed my potato latkes and homemade applesauce at Hanukah, said the blessings over the candles and told me how yummy my cinnamon rolls are while we open all the goodies in our Christmas stockings. They have gone to the temples in Bali with me and honored offerings. They know I believe in some type of life after death and are on their own searches as well.

• • •

Dad,

I have been a seeker since mom passed away, trying to under-stand death and dying.

I have read, listened, meditated since your death, trying to discov-er the beliefs that fit.

Do you have anything to share?

Karen,

We are all on our own journey.

We all seek to know and understand.

Find what comforts you.

Find what will help you be ready.

Find what will help you live the days you have.

I was ready, know that.

So, do all, see all, feel all, so you are ready like I was.

Trust in your own journey.

I believe in your seeking.

I believe you will discover what is meant for you.

Dad,

In April, about four months after your passing, I went to Sedona.

I felt so many interesting connections to you there.

Shangri-La, your favorite film, was the name of the center I en-gaged in for all activities.

A Masonic Temple stood next to a labyrinth I walked one early morning.

Max Brand and Louis L'Amour, your favorite Western authors, lived and wrote in Sedona.

A huge high-back arm chair was carved in the mountain rocks I walked past at sunset one evening.

Dad you were there with me.

Karen,

In Sedona you allowed your heart to open and begin to accept my death.

You were on auto pilot from December 1st until then.

You planned my funeral, took care of the house and my belongings.

You showed up at your work each day and never let them see your sadness and hurt.

Sedona opened the opportunity for you to start grieving.

Of course, I knew Max Brand and Louis wrote in Sedona.

They were great adventurers.

I loved seeing the world through their words.

NOT ONLY DID MY dad love to read Westerns but he loved watching all the John Wayne cowboy and adventure movies. He also told me that he learned a great deal about history through reading those books. Those writers were known for revealing true facts about those incredible times.

Sedona allowed my tears to flow.

Sedona confirmed that there was something greater than coincidence working in life.

I had been on automatic pilot. I was devastated losing my dad. It was the hardest thing I had ever gone through in my life.

• • •

Dad,

If you were here, what advice would you give me?

How would you say to live my life?

What encouragement would you offer?

What made you happy about the life you led?

What helped you always be there for us?

Was it gratitude?

Honey,

My advice has always been:

Get all the education you can.

You will be a woman competing in a man's world.

Never be afraid to ask for what you need.

**Celebrate your birthday, even if you have to throw yourself
a party.**

Celebrate each day you have to live another day.

Thank those who give life.

Karen, yes, BE GRATEFUL

MY DAD SEEMED TO regret that he was never able to obtain a
college degree. He had to go to work right out of high school.
His family was not able to support continuing his education.
It was important that my brother and I go to college and obtain
that next level of knowledge. He always felt it would provide us
with greater opportunities in life.

My father didn't need that degree. He had something that
doesn't come from taking courses—it comes from understanding
who you are and leading with your heart. Even the day before
he died, he reaffirmed that he had lived a great life and accomplished much. I believe he knew he'd been the best husband he

could, the best brother he could and the best father he could.

. . .

Dad,

It's a new day and I'm thinking of you of course.

I have returned from enjoying my chai latte with friends. I like coconut milk in mine and I like it very hot. The way you enjoyed your tea.

Dad, you got up each morning and prepared your cereal in a very careful manner. You took down a ceramic bowl from the kitchen cabinets and pulled out a silver spoon from the drawer next to the refrigerator. You poured in your Maxie Mix (two or three cereals combined).

You put your tea mug on the counter and put one Lipton tea bag in the cup, turned on the gas stove and placed the tea kettle of water on to boil.

Then you walked across the hall back to the bathroom and shaved.

When you heard the whistle of the kettle you walked back into the kitchen and turned it off. You poured water into your mug, and returned to your room to dress while the tea seeped. There was a slice of lemon beside the mug for use later.

You always wore slacks, a t-shirt and over-shirt.

You always had soft socks. You put on your shoes using a shoe horn, never to hurt the backs of your shoes.

You really cared about everything you owned.

Honey,
My parents worked hard.
I worked hard.

I took care of things because they didn't come easy and I respected that.

I did not live beyond my capabilities.

I enjoyed what I had.

I DON'T THINK MY dad ever lived beyond his means. He paid cash for everything, except his home, for which he was sure to write the mortgage check every month, neatly and accurately with all the account numbers. He even had a safe that he kept in the downstairs closet with a bit of extra cash. I remember on many occasions he would travel down the steps and come back with some fresh one hundred dollars bills just for me to do something fun. I think the safe was his idea of keeping money under the mattress for a raining day.

· · ·

Dad,

Now, I understand apricot jam spooned into your tea.

I understand brown sugar on your oatmeal with raisins.

I understand cinnamon and sugar and lots of butter on your matzo brei.

It's sweetness in daily life.

Yes, Honey
Either find sweetness each day or add it.

Dad,

It's the little caring things you always did.

Setting up and tearing down all the holiday tables and chairs.

Doing all the dishes after mom planned and cooked and served us.

There was also the vacuuming after the family had all enjoyed crab and turkey.

Karen,
Your mom worked hard.
I worked hard.
We shared responsibility.
I would never take advantage of anyone.
No one should.
I enjoyed doing my part to help.
I also liked doing some things in the way I liked them to be done and completed.

MY DAD WAS VERY generous and thoughtful. I remember the times he took my cousins out shopping at the Emporium on Market Street in San Francisco, just to help them look great for a new job or interview or because it was their birthday. He thought it was fun to take us out on his birthday and buy presents for us. He never forgot my mom's birthday or their anniversary. He loved buying those really, really large cards for her with arms that popped out offering hugs.

He appreciated the things my mom did and never took her for granted.

• • •

Dad,

It was also the BIG things you did:

Reading the Wizard of Oz to me at bed time,

A helicopter ride to Disneyland,

The dances you helped me plan at Lowell High School,

And the dances you taught me to do.

Most of all, you believed in my abilities.

Karen,

I enjoyed making you happy.

I enjoyed new ideas.

I liked creating.

I enjoyed seeing you enjoy life.

I always believed in you.

I COULD DEPEND UPON my dad. He never really let me down. I had wished, one time, he would stand up to my mom, but he showed me how shooting anger back at someone doesn't really benefit in the end. In hind sight, I guess he stood up for what was truly important to him; time to go to the forty-niner games, living in the city he wanted, work, driving the car he wanted, supporting his sisters, reading the books he was passionate about reading, staying involved in the Masonic Lodge and seeing his kids succeed.

. . .

Dad,

Were you ever sad?

I don't remember seeing you sad.

I saw joy and laughter, especially when you saw a
Peter Sellers film.

Were you ever distracted?

I saw focus and attention especially if we were talking or you were doing the books for the pawnshop.

I think I saw pain when you were recovering from surgery, but I watched you conquer that and work to heal yourself.

Karen,

I don't think the men of my time were encouraged to show a variety of feelings, especially those of sadness.

I know you saw me get mad.

Remember when I threw that customer out of the pawnshop for disrespecting my faith and threatening your brother's well-being?

I don't remember being distracted.... hmmm guess I was in fact a focused man.

Honey, pain, we all experience pain;

Pain of body,

Pain of loss.

You just have to work through it.

Feelings change all the time.

I DON'T THINK MY dad saw problems as complex. I think actions were either right or wrong for him. I think he accepted what he could accept and found other ways to handle what he could not. He didn't get drunk. He did however enjoy a vodka and orange juice once in a while or a vodka and tonic on the shaker. He didn't smoke. When he thought he was getting a bit over weight, he stopped using ketchup and decreased the jam, a bit, that he put in his tea. When the doctors told him to watch the sugar, he read the labels on everything and ate accordingly. He followed all instructions after his heart surgery and was back at work as soon as he could walk a block on his own.

. . .

Dad,

My sons miss you.

Josh remembers the Herb Caen article that appeared in the *SF Examiner* about your guy's trip to the Super Bowl together. I think he was about nine or ten years old.

You guys flew all the way to Miami and met Herb Caen on the flight.

Herb thought it was really special that you were taking your grandson to the big game.

It was something Joshua has never forgotten. The Leroy Niemen painting of that game hangs in his home.

Your yellow leather kitchen chairs still adorn Joshua's kitchen in his house in Roseville as well.

You know, all three boys wear your tie tacks and cuff links.

They remember their trip with you on the cruise and their time fishing with you in Hawaii.

They remember the one hundred dollar bills you gave them for gas when they drove to see you.

Honey,

When you have the ability to give, then give.

I enjoyed seeing your boy's eyes widen when they held those one hundred-dollar bills.

Nothing gave me more pleasure than seeing your sons enjoy our times together.

I have seen Josh fall asleep in my old comfy chair.

It's a good feeling when someone wants to connect with their family.

It's a good feeling when someone you love wants to be close.

MY DAD LOVED HIS family. He would do anything for them. He also had standards. When my brother flunked out of UC Berkeley, he told him to go to City College, get a job, move home and pay for his own gas. My brother worked really hard one semester and was back at college in no time.

He listened to my three sons. He also expected them to behave in public, respect their mother and finish college. He was so excited to take Josh, the eldest to the Super Bowl. He was excited to show him off to his Aunt Becky who lived in Florida half the year. He was also so impressed when Herb Caen wrote about a special grandpa taking his grandson to the game. He kept that article pinned up in the pawnshop.

He got such a kick out the boys catching one of those big fish off the boat in Hawaii. You'd have thought he caught the fish. Fishing was the only leisure activity other than football I can remember my father enjoying.

• • •

Dad,

Do you see me?

Was there a time you were still present here but not to my eyes?

Do you feel?

Do you still have all your memories of your life?

Did you meet your mom, dad or my mom, Jeanie, Ruthie or Sammy?

Karen,

There are some things you will have to wait to know.

I know you have read books.

You have seen films.

You have been to Spirit Rock for spiritual practices.

What do you want to believe?

Believe what feels right to you.

The unknown is the unknown until you know.

So, until you know Karen, be open.

MY DAD WAS A private man. He didn't share about how he felt or what he believed for himself. He encouraged us to get an education, to travel and think anything was possible. We didn't talk about his mom, dad or his sister after their deaths. We didn't visit the cemetery after their burials. But each year on each of their birthdays or passing anniversary, he would drive to Safeway and purchase a Yahrzeit Candle, honoring each of them. This was a Jewish memorial candle, which stayed lit for twenty-four hours. I wonder what he said to himself when he lit them? I know that when I purchase mine honoring him, yes from Safeway, I acknowledge my gratitude and love and my hope to see him once again in the next life.

. . .

Life Memories Recalled

Dad,

I miss your Sunday morning Matzo Brei.

You made the best matzo pancake in the whole world with just the right amount of butter, sugar and, of course, cinnamon.

Karen,

Just remember you can buy matzo any time, don't wait for Passover.

Just soak it good in your egg mixture.

Use more butter than you think.

Let it get golden brown on one side.

Then flip.

Add butter if you need to.

When the second side is golden brown, you are done.

Mix cinnamon with sugar and nicely coat the top of your pancake.

Some apricot jam is good to add.

Be sure to use a good frying pan, not too big.

Make pancakes one at a time.

Think of me each time.

"So, SHALL I MAKE us a Matzo Brei?" asked my dad, usually on a Sunday morning. He was always so excited to make something for me. Then we enjoyed our meal together. I don't really think we had any in depth conversations. He would read the Sunday paper and I would enjoy a hot yummy pancake with sugar and cinnamon. The pancake simply connected us in the moment. I think that is why I enjoy making homemade hot cinnamon rolls on Christmas morning and sharing them with my sons. This is pure sweetness in life, for sure.

Dad,

Do you recall when we fished off Tiburon Pier?

You showed me the eggs inside the womb of the fish.

Do you also remember when we drove to Rodeo to fish off Captain Charlie's boat?

You said, "Whatever you get on your hook is yours to bring in."

It was a shark — pretty darn large.

Well, I brought it in, all on my own.

Those fishing lessons of wisdom remain with me today.

Thanks.

Karen,

You know, I enjoyed fishing a great deal.

I loved sharing those times with you and your mom.

There are wisdoms everywhere.

Just see.

Just ask.

Just listen.

Happy to know that I showed you how simple things like fishing can help you understand and live in the world.

THAT MEMORY HAS ALWAYS stuck with me. Dad was, in his way, saying, "You can do this." He was building my confidence. It was also a time my mom and dad and I shared some type of activity together. Come to think of it, there was contentment for all of us on those fishing trips.

. . .

Dad,

I was thinking about the time you flew down to Arizona State University, just after I had finished my Bachelor's Degree.

You said, "Don't come home yet, get your Master's Degree".

That is what I did. You were so wise.

You encouraged at just the right time.

You always made me feel safe and loved and believed in.

I miss feeling taken care of like that.

I was so lucky. Thank you.

Honey,

Education was one of the most important things to me.

I felt it was the key to having choices in life.

I wanted you and your brother to have as many as possible.

I wanted you both to have doors open to you.

I wished you had stayed and obtained your PhD.

I always told you that a woman must have more than a man to compete in this world.

I know later you thought about going back.

I think life with the boys was however more important for you and having to start all over again, after losing your school, took all your love, time and energy and that PHD wasn't possible.

It is okay, you did so many other amazing things with your knowledge that made differences in lives.

THIS QUESTION BROUGHT UP sadness for me. I wish my father was still here so I could share more of my life. I hope he saw my work in Bali and Uganda. I hope he saw my first published book. I hope he saw my work with Wings Learning Center, helping them create a well-respected and effective school for those with autism.

33

I really hope my mom saw my published book, *On the Yellow Brick Road*. I frustrated her with my spelling errors and illegible handwriting as a child. I think she would have been proud.

• • •

Dad,

I was driving down highway 101 towards the city, going over the Golden Gate Bridge and I was thinking about your 1960's forest green Mustang with its black leather seats.

I remember the day you were in the basement of our home on 33rd avenue installing the special horn that sounded like a small horse.

I remember your smile. That horn tickled your fancy. Such a little thing gave you such grand satisfaction.

You got such a kick out of showing that horn to others.

You were playful.

It is good to be playful.

I need to make more playful times in my life.

Karen,

I wish I had played more.

I had family to think about.

My parents needed my help.

My sister, Jean, needed my help.

I wanted you and your brother to have opportunities.

That brought me happiness.

But, please play.

Dress funny.

Dress colorful.

Dance more.

See more.

See plays and hear concerts if you like.

Read.

But find playfulness in each day.

MY DAD WAS A man of simple needs. He loved to dance. His face lit up. His feet were so light and moved so gracefully across the dance floor. He wanted to be on stage but his mother and father said it was no career for a Jewish man. He wanted to be part of vaudeville. He made a doll that strapped on your feet and it became his partner.

He didn't talk much about this time in his life. I believe he honored and valued his parents' thoughts and beliefs. I also don't believe he had much choice or encouragement to follow this interest.

So, he developed other interests, like reading those Westerns, fishing, supporting the 49ers and joining the Masons and helping his family.

I do wonder how his life would have been if he had lived that dream. Near the end of his life, my father told me, he had no regrets. He had lived a good life.

· · ·

Dad,

I was thinking about all the times you helped me make my quota on those campfire mint sales.

I think I was the only campfire girl to hit all the pawnshops in San Francisco.

I remember receiving my patch or special beads each time.

I remember you sewing them on my blue felt vest.

Wow, you were a darn good seamstress!

35

You seemed to support me in so many ways.

You were so versatile.

Who showed you how to be such a wonderful father?

Karen,

My father came from the old country of Russia which was sometimes Poland.

Family mattered to him.

Taking care of the family mattered.

He was a strong patriarch.

My mother tempered him, but in a strong way.

My dad had only brothers.

My mom only sisters.

Yin & Yang, like you say these days was in my blood.

It didn't matter.

Family was family.

We didn't seem to be so caught up in this male vs female.

I think I just took what felt right from each one of them.

I guess you benefited from my ability to be open to what my father offered as well as my mother's strengths.

I am not sure if I thought I was a good father but I know that I tried to do my best to support you and your brother.

Thank you for giving me the opportunity.

I was grateful to have you and your brother so I could practice being the best father I could.

Dad,

You had very specific strategies for getting things accomplished.

There was the precise way you liked the suits in our pawnshop dusted off before putting them on the sales rack.

Left shoulder, right shoulder, down the backside, left sleeve, right sleeve, font left, right front and then done.

Back on the hanger the item went.

I wonder if some of my organizational strengths for directing schools came from observing your systems.

Honey,

We all have our preferred ways of doing things.

It is what gives us a sense of security and control.

I did have my ways and those ways were even more important as I aged.

I liked my tea boiled, not microwaved. I did think it tasted different.

I had my preferred ways of driving to places and I did want everyone to drive those exact ways.

I liked familiar.

There was comfort.

Systems helped.

Systems build consistency.

I am sure in your work with children with autism, consistency is important.

I HAD A GREAT DEAL of respect for my father. I think he respected me, for who I am, not what someone thinks I should be. I think his up-bringing enabled him to encourage me to access both the female and male sides of my personality. As I said, he worked six days a week and I think he just wanted to be part of my life, so when he saw an opportunity to support me, he did. The Blue Birds, the Campfire girls, and my high school vice presidency were great opportunities for him to engage.

. . .

Dad,

I was passing Sutter Hospital here in Novato and a memory flashed in my mind.

It was the day you had my brother Darryl and I meet you at the hospital, where mom was. We were to meet up with Dr. Mackler, mom's doctor, in one of the small offices provided on patient floors.

Mom was not doing well.

We all knew it was time to let her go.

Medicine couldn't help her.

Surgery wasn't an option.

She was on life support, but not truly living life.

You looked the two of us straight in the eyes and motioned towards us with your finger.

"I am making this decision," you said. "This is my decision," you repeated. "We are bringing Mom home to die in her own home, in her own bedroom, in her own bed."

Once again, you were thinking of us.

You were making sure we did not blame ourselves.

Once again, your wisdom radiated.

How did you become so wise?

Karen,

I was born in 1914. I lived 90 years

In those years of living, I sure hope I gained some wisdom.

Karen, I continue to emphasize, family matters.

Being a father means making sure your children are safe.

It just was the right words for me.

It was my responsibility.

Husbands and wives have to make hard decisions.

Some not appreciated.

Some not comfortable.

Some perhaps not right.

But we try our best.

Your mom's time in the physical was coming to an end.

Her body could not express her any longer.

Pain needed to be over.

It was time for all of us to let her be relieved from the hardships of the body.

MY BROTHER AND I never questioned his decision. He was right. He was wise. My brother was quiet. I hope I always will find ways to help my sons live with as little regret as possible. I hope each of us can understand that we are not perfect. We do our best. We try. Sometimes we just need to surrender and let go.

• • •

Dad,

"By the rough ashlar founded in the quarry" was a phrase you had to practice over and over again when studying for your Masonic degrees. I remember sitting on the large sectional in the living room coaching you (ha, really just listening as you learned those important words).

You were committed. You took your membership in this fraternal group seriously.

I think you set a great example for me, to make sure that when I joined anything or committed to something, that I gave it all I had.

A commitment is a sign of trustworthiness, you said.

You had great values. Thank you.

Karen,

When you say yes to someone, a group, a project, an idea, a change, it is wise to uphold your yes.

So, research first.

Make sure it aligns with your beliefs.

Make sure you can follow through with it.

Make sure it does not hurt another.

Trust works both ways.

So, at any point in the yes that you find out the idea, project, person or group no longer aligns, it's time for the NO.

That's it.

No regrets.

Be open to what is next.

Move on.

WHEN I WAS GOING through a very difficult time, divorce and losing a school I had dreamed of, built and directed for 20 years, my father's words were always in my mind. I would try as hard as I could to make the marriage work. I would do anything that aligned with my values and beliefs. Then it was over. I had to let go. I had to start over. I would do everything I knew how to keep my school but when the students and their families could be in harm, I had to say no. I had to be open to what was next. It was hard, but I moved on.

· · ·

Heh Dad,

Just thinking about prom time at my school in Redwood City. Each year we put on a prom so the students with autism can enjoy the same type of social event their typical peer enjoys but designed to support them.

I remember when you encouraged me to think outside the box on designing and implementing dances at Lowell High school when I was vice president of the school.

You encouraged me to stand up to the administration and suggest singles be able to attend the dances instead of couples only. You encouraged me to promote three bands not one and have music all the time instead of breaks.

Thanks for encouraging me to mix it up, do something different and not to be afraid to suggest different ideas to the powers that be.

Karen,

I was proud you ran for office and enjoyed helping you.

It gave me an opportunity to do things with you that I enjoyed doing as well.

Leaders see what is, listen and make things better.

You did.

MY DAD WAS OPTIMISTIC. He thought things were possible. He taught me to just ask. I would never have opened up a residential school, for children with autism, had it not been for his encouragement to believe in myself and to think things were possible. There were so many who said, it's too hard, laws are too restrictive, it's too costly and are you really sure, with a scowl on their face. I wanted to make things better for the child with autism. So, I listened and saw the possibilities and I found ways to resolve the challenges.

• • •

Dad,

You loved volunteering to help at events.

You volunteered to help mom at all her Eastern Star events at that center on Brotherhood way in the city.

Game night was a fun event that you facilitated.

Blintz Breakfasts were a time guests enjoyed your Ramos fizzes and Gin Fizzes for three hundred people.

You were always making people comfortable and happy.

You were all about creating fun for people.

Kindness and service are your attributes I have always tried to live by.

Honey,

I did love creating fun activities.

I liked people.

I tried to see the good in each person.

I tried not to judge a book by its cover.

What people wore, did for a living weren't the important things that mattered.

Who they were as an individual, was.

Kindness, loyalty, trustworthiness are good attributes.

Remember everyone has a story.

We just don't know it until we take the time to hear it.

Do not be quick to judge.

MY DAD HELPED EVERYONE who came into his pawnshop, except those who disrespected my brother or him. He loaned on a pair of shoes, an overcoat, leather goods, of course, jewelry and instruments, but he tried to loan on whatever the customer thought of value. My dad didn't dress up to go to work. He dressed comfortably. He dressed warm, on cold days. He wore different colored Pendleton shirts, heavy working pants and this odd beanie on his head. He even wore it to I. Magnin, one of the fanciest stores in San Francisco. He often had to wait for someone to wait on him, due to their perception that a man of his adornment couldn't possibly afford to purchase his wife's birthday gift here. Don't be too quick to judge.

· · ·

Dad,

I am reminded by two pieces of wisdom you gave me during my divorce:

Get the toughest attorney possible.

Don't be possessed by your possessions.

You wanted me protected. You wanted me to also find a way to let go and consider what is truly important.

Things, not so much.

Feelings, very much.

Peace of mind, oh, yes.

Karen,

Your divorce was one of the toughest times of your life.

I was angry at your ex for not being grateful and more compassionate.

I wanted you to obtain what you were entitled to and you worked so hard to create.

I thought getting the toughest legal advisor was the way to go.

But honey when the writing was on the wall, that you were going to lose, so unfairly, what you deserved, I wanted you to let go.

I wanted you to move on and begin to heal.

Fighting maintains anger.

Anger hurts the heart.

A building, furniture, objects are not so important.

No one could ever take away your knowledge, your caring, and your passion.

I just hoped more would come to you in the future.

I DID MOVE ON. I learned to forgive. I let go of possessions. I kept my knowledge; with my passion I went on to help others in different ways. It was hard, but dad was right on, once again.

. . .

Dad,

One of the last days of your life with me, I walked into the TV room and heard you call out to your mom. You said, "Cecilia".

Did you see your mother that moment?

Did you hear her?

Did she in some way help you transition?

Will you be there for me?

Honey,

If I called my mother's name out, then she was in my heart's eye.

I doubt you would have heard me say anything if she wasn't right there.

Her name was always comforting to me.

I always missed her.

I loved her.

If I am supposed to be there when you transition, I will be.

MY DAD WAS ALWAYS hopeful. He wanted me to think things were possible. I remember the hospice ladies saying that they saw my dad lift his arms up and then he was gone. I hope Cecilia was there. My father deserved to have that experience. He provided comfort and guidance to his family, always.

. . .

Guidance for Living

Dad,

Did you see the four masked gunmen come into the pawnshop during this past Christmas holiday?

Was it you who made sure my brother didn't die that day?

Did you see him reach for the loaded gun you left in the metal file cabinet in case of an emergency?

That gun had to be thirty plus years old.

He never got a shot off.

That masked gunman rapid fired and those bullets bounced off every piece of metal in the back room, straight through Darryl's right and left hands, and then one lodged in his backside. The gunman just ran out of there with the other three, never to be seen again.

Was it your energy that helped him get himself to the desk chair and wait for the 911 call to be answered?

Did you follow him to San Francisco General Hospital watching over his surgery?

My brother has so much strength within him.

I didn't lose him that day. I am so grateful.

Karen,
I am always with you and your brother.
It wasn't time for your brother to leave.
He has more life to live.
Please remind him.
He too should send his birthday cards to his surgery team thanking them for each year of life he will receive going forward.
Your brother is strong and kind and generous and smart
Enjoy time with him.

Dad,

I am more worried about my brother since the shooting.

Please look out for him.

He needs your wisdom more than ever.

What would you advise him to do with the next stage of his physical life, now that he must close the pawnshop?

It was hard for him to put the sign in the window of the pawnshop. "No Loans, Redemptions Only."

A pawnshop is a place of loaning and redeeming.

How do I support him?

How do we all help him find the way or must he do it alone?

Honey,

I always gave your brother the space he needed to make his own decisions.

Remember, I said there could only be one boss in the pawnshop and then I stepped back.

Just show him you care.

Just be there when he reaches out.

Just check in on him like you do every Wednesday. Your humpday check in is perfect.

You guys have been doing that for nearly two decades.

He knows you love and appreciate him.

SOMEONE OR SOMETHING WAS watching over my brother that day. It is amazing he wasn't killed. It's hard to see someone you love suffer. It is hard to see someone who has always been generous to others lose something so important to him because he is worried about keeping everyone else safe. I believe it is important to let those you love, know it. Life can be taken from us instantly.

47

I will also respect my dad's advice. I will be there. I will continue to show him I care. I will acknowledge his anger and sadness and find ways to let him know I am present for him.

. . .

Dad,

When Darryl put up the "No Loans, Only Redemptions" sign, I was sad.

I thought about all the memories in the pawnshop and all the stories.

I thought, perhaps I should gather up some memorabilia each time I go to the store.

My first items were a few of the old pawn ticket books you made out of pieces of left-over cardboard.

Darryl pointed to all the boxes you made to hold supplies like rubber bands, envelopes and cards.

We giggled at the cash drawer holder. We could see the actual bottom of the drawer now, as some of the slots had worn thin.

Dad, you bought these heavy-duty metal scotch tape holders. We found four of them and Darryl thinks there may be more. They must be thirty years old and still doing their job. I am thinking of using them as book ends.

Dad, your special hand broom is now in my garage. Cousin Scott gave it to me the last time I was at the store. It was hanging in the back room of the pawnshop. Not sure it was getting much use.

You were always making sure the store was organized and clean.

I have to tell you, no one cared as much as you about making do with what you had, buying things that lasted, or keeping things clean and organized.

But I also must tell you that Darryl never threw out anything you created.

I think it made him feel your presence.

Your desk is still organized just the way you left it. He works at it the way you did.

Dad, do you think we all have keepsakes around to help us feel closer to those who have moved on?

Karen,

Good to know the things I made by hand have lasted all these years.

I was proud to create useful items.

I also bought things that would last.

I can't understand why these days, manufacturer's only make things to last a short time. Where are they putting all those broken items?

Your mom's washer lasted twenty years.

I used my car-drying chamois over and over again, until there were no more threads to hold on to.

We need to be careful. To recycle, to re-purpose and re-use whenever we can.

Karen, you know I kept a few special pictures in my alligator wallet. It was a picture of my mom and dad, a picture of you and Darryl when you were young and one of your mom when we first married.

Guess we each decide what to keep close to us at all times.

I REMEMBER THOSE PICTURES, matter of fact I still have my dad's wallet with the last dollars he had in it and those sentimental pictures. My mom bought that wallet for him. She too knew how to buy things that would last. I think my dad would be very disappointed in the way things are made now, definitely not to last. When my father passed away, I had to throw out all the twisters that you would find in boxes of plastic bags. He must have saved all

49

of them from all the boxes he purchased over twenty plus years or so. I also had to unravel disintegrating rubber bands wrapped around several door knobs in his home and throw them out. I remember dad saved the roller skates I had out grown and turned them into the wheels on my homemade coaster he made. I giggled when I saw one of his homemade boxes in the pawnshop filled with more rubber bands than anyone could use in years. So, I took those bands of many sizes and shapes and turned them into stretch awards for my school staff at the end of the school year.

. . .

Dad,

I was up at Mendocino for my 67th birthday. The boys scheduled the trip and the activities. It was a beautiful drive up the coast. The town of Mendocino is quaint. You'd like it. Fun little shops to stroll through, nice cafés to eat in and beautiful north coast beaches to walk. Tyler is thinking of getting married there in 2019, in a Cypress Grove overlooking the ocean. You would enjoy that wedding. Please look in. Anyway, on the way back, Sean took me on highway 128, a great scenic road of wineries, ranches, restaurants, quirky shops and some fruit stands.

We stopped and bought some yummy apples.

Today while peeling those apples to make applesauce, I giggled.

I remembered your ritual for preparing your apple and cheese for you evening dessert, of course, with your cup of Lipton tea with its fresh lemon slice.

You peeled off the skin of the apple in one continuous round chain. You twisted the stem off the apple next.

Then you took out that metal apple slicer. I could never center that tool.

You had just the right touch.

You took out a rectangular brick of Monterey Jack cheese from the refrigerator and sliced one perfect slice for each apple, sliced by that metal thing.

All the while your water for your tea was boiling in the tea kettle.

Then you tore off one, no, I think two pieces of paper towel sheets.

Then you enjoyed your favorite TV show or football game, crunching and sipping.

Karen,

About the apples:

I enjoyed the simple things in life.

I found comfort in preparation.

I appreciated the crisp apple taste and my soothing hot tea.

Yes.

WE WILL ALL MISS my Dad, Papa Max, in the cypress grove in 2019, but somehow, he will be in our hearts. I just know it. Maybe we will enjoy some apples that weekend. The wedding is in the fall when the apples have come perfectly into season.

. . .

Dad,

You are not going believe this.

Today, I went out to my writing space.

I was ready to type my question to you.

I didn't realize I was typing on the typewriter you use to communicate with me

The ribbon got stuck.

My fingers were covered in ink, trying to realign the ribbon.

Do you think I messed up the energy by typing to you on your typewriter?

Do you think the typewriter was trying to tell me, "Not this one?"

Karen,

Interesting.

I don't know what happened with the typewriter ribbon.

I don't think it matters which you use or I use.

You experience the physical sense of typing on the machine.

I don't.

The words, the thoughts, the conversation matters.

I am just sending my responses in words to you so you can tap them out.

Just keep on typing.

Maybe you need a new ribbon, that's all.

Unless of course, it does matter!

I TRIED TO FIX that ribbon that day. It wasn't cooperating. I took a deep breath and accepted that I could type to my dad on the Royal. I realized that life is again about letting go, surrendering to what isn't working and establishing a state of wonder. I realized

I need to be more open to what might be just around the corner, what could happen if I tried something new instead of maintaining old patterns and to risk more.

. . .

Dad,

Do you feel loneliness where you are?

Did you feel loneliness when you lived in my physical world?

Karen,

I will always miss my time with you, but something happens when we leave and I do not relate to loneliness here.

I didn't think about loneliness when I was your father.

I had my work. I had my books. I had you and your brother and your kids to celebrate with.

I enjoyed movies, eating out and belonging to the Masons and the Eastern Star.

I enjoyed planning trips.

I don't think I made room for loneliness.

I am so sorry you are feeling lonely.

Are you sure it is loneliness?

Find happiness. Make happy moments. Realize not every moment can be happy.

I GUESS MY DAD was content, not just calm. I realized he did accept his life. I realized that he was satisfied with all he had. He lived for his present moments. Today there is a great deal of energy around mindfulness. I think my dad would have agreed with this movement.

. . .

Dad,

Getting older has been one of those thoughts on mind my since I reached sixty years of age.

I have been wondering how to gracefully and with wisdom enter these older years, knowing I do not have sixty more years, unless a miracle occurs.

As a child I never considered old age.

I accepted your aging.

I just didn't think you would ever be gone from my life.

Did you accept aging?

Did you dwell on it?

Karen,

I never shared with you much of my inner feelings.

It wasn't the natural thing to do in my time.

I was your father. My job was to provide support to you and not find support in you.

Later in life I let you know a few things about my feelings and I know you heard them.

Enjoy the life you have. Yes, you may not have one hundred and twenty years.

But you can make every day count until the very last.

Laugh, eat delicious food, see different places in the world and read.

Enjoy family.

Don't think of aging, just take care of yourself as you live each day.

Get to a point where you are ready to let go when aging in this life ends.

As I have said before, I was ready.

No regrets, I say.

Karen,

I am so sorry honey.

I am not sure any of us imagine what life will feel like when our parents are gone.

We know we will miss them. We know life will be different.

We seem to know, no one lives forever yet we just go on with our daily lives acting as if they will.

Honey, I will always be in your heart.

I will always be available to have conversations.

MY CONVERSATIONS WITH MY father have shown me that I can have time with him any time I wish. I can pick up a pencil or pen or open a typewriter and just fire questions away or make comments to him. I know I will receive from him. I know what it is like to be here, in this life, without the physical presence of my dad. I understand no one lives forever and I will show gratitude for every day I have and that I had with my dad. I will try not to miss opportunities, in this physical life, that I have been given. I will attempt to have no regrets and I will access every means to keep in excellent health, attempting to age gracefully.

. . .

Dad,

I don't ever remember you deciding what I should do or be as an adult or pressuring me to go into one area or another.

Get a good education was your mantra, but not do, be or become something you wanted me to become.

I remember you telling me that your parents said NO to you on becoming an entertainer. I believe they said it wasn't something a Jewish man should do.

I never asked you how you felt about that. I'm sorry.

Karen

I think my mother and father did not want me to be on the road. I think they wanted me close by.

I enjoyed my time managing the department store on Market Street. I got to travel, I trimmed windows, connected with customers and determined product need. I was successful.

I enjoyed the pawn-broking business as well. It taught me a great deal about the value of items and it made a good living for our family. That seemed to be enough for me.

My only wish was that I might have been given an opportunity to have more education. I am not sure what paths I could have taken with more education.

I WAS LUCKY TO HAVE a dad who encouraged me to pursue my interests. I was lucky to have a dad that could financially support my obtaining a post-secondary degree and master's degree. I was lucky I had a dad who was invested in my happiness. He is my hero. It is his wisdoms that I try to emulate. It is his actions that I try to model with my sons. I am grateful for who he was, not what he might have been.

My dad needed to go to work right after high school. He needed to help his parents. He needed to make his own living. My grandfather was a painter. My grandmother was a stay at home mom but when my grandfather opened up a second hand store, my grandmother worked side by side with him in the shop on Folsom in San Francisco. They lived in a flat in San Francisco. They had one car and lived a simple life.

. . .

Dad,

I remember you trying to teach me to dance.

I loved dancing with you. Your guidance on the floor was soft and direct.

I could feel your hand guiding my back in the various directions.

You were a guide in so many ways in my life. I appreciate that.

Thank you.

Dad,

By the way, you were right. It doesn't matter which typewriter I use.

Our channels are open.

Words seem to flow just fine.

Answers are heard clearly.

Sometimes I can just think the thought or question in my head and your wisdoms come.

Honey,

I told you I am always with you.

Just ask and then listen.

WE ALL NEED GUIDANCE in our lives. Guidance comes in all types of forms. We can find wisdom in a book. We can find wisdom in a movie. We can receive guidance from a parent, sibling, aunt or uncle, friend, teacher, spiritual mentor or obtain it from an experience. We have those who teach us how to love and support. We have others who teach us how to be strong and defend ourselves. We have those who show us how we don't want to be and what we don't ever want to do again. Surround yourself with those who guide you according to your special values and beliefs. Find heroes who lead with their heart.

. . .

Dad, one more question –

What do you think about all this technology?

Karen,

I am sure there is a purpose to some of it, but I will tell you it was not to my liking.

It seems that while it brings everyone all the world together fast, it puts distance between people as well.

I believe it's rude when people talk on the phone while at the grocery store having their items checked in.

I think it's sad to see people out for dinner, looking at their phones instead of telling each other stories about their day.

It frustrated me when I couldn't actually speak to someone on the phone without following so many commands and pressing so many numbers before, I could reach someone.

I think you remember that the cell phone, the one your brother gave me, well it didn't work too well with me. I never kept it with me. I never turned it on except when I was in the car, charging it. Not very helpful to others.

I have watched technology become the connection between the young, the young and their family and learning in schools.

I just hope the world can find a balance.

I hope people can turn off their technology every now and then and go fishing, read to their children, or enjoy the taste of their meal and get lost in a good book instead of U-Tube videos.

IF MY DAD WAS frustrated with never being able to talk to a real person, when he was alive, he'd be cursing at what happens now. He would wonder where service went. He would wonder why the customer was no longer important. He would be overwhelmed with not being able understand those on the phone because they were actually in India and had no idea of the culture, he lived in. He wouldn't understand waiting forty-five plus minutes on the phone to resolve a problem or someone taking his number to call him back when a time spot opened up. He would not like his grandchildren more engaged in Facebook than learning to fish.

• • •

Dad,

Your wisdoms moved me to action.

I took my books on aging with grace, life after death stories, it's okay to be alone and finding my true self, out of the book shelf and took them directly to the used book store.

Wow, I felt so much lighter. I am finished reading about death, after-life, dying and finding my true self.

I also made a trip to Goodwill with clothing that just didn't compliment me any longer.

The recycle bin in the garage also filled up quickly with all kinds of paper work and duplicate documents, I was saving for what or who, I don't know.

As you suggested, I am just going to stop re-reading and re-thinking about the future and just do more living.

Dad,

I realize the typewriters were brought into my life to reaffirm you are always with me.

I realized I didn't need to feel alone. I didn't need to read any more about dying gracefully or imagining what the next life would be.

I was stuck, dad.

Tapping to you, helped.

I am moving forward these days.

It's a good thing.

Thank you. Grateful always.

Honey,

I am so glad you are realizing you just need to make this life happen and not worry about the next or what has passed.

MAKING THIS LIFE COUNT is not just my father's recommendation, but mine too, to anyone reading these conversations. I can bet that if you speak to anyone who has passed, they wouldn't say work more, buy more, they would say laugh more, see more, wonder more, love more, hug more, enjoy long walks with friends or family, read more, wear purple if you like, even in your hair.

• • •

Final Taps

Dad,

I hope my sons will connect with me when I am no longer physically in their lives.

My plan is to read *Typewriters to Heaven and Back* to them.

Perhaps, it will help them realize I will always be with them and that they might write to me, type to me, take a walk on the beach and talk to me and then: wait, listen, see what their mom would advise.

Perhaps, it will make them feel a bit more connected, as I have felt to you during our tapping times.

I will leave the Royal Typewriter, safely packed in its case for them to discover.

Perhaps it will call out to one of them.

Who knows?

I hope others, who read *Typewriters to Heaven and Back* might find it helpful for them to get moving forward. Maybe it will help them to know that those who have loved them are always in their hearts and ready to receive thoughts and questions.

Maybe they will come across a special typewriter at an antique store, flea market or garage sale, and they might hear, "Start Tapping to Me." "I am waiting to hear from you."

Love you always, Dad.

Karen

Honey,

I like your idea of reading our conversations to the boys.

It brings me closer to them as well.

I am here, wishing you a life well lived.

Dance more.

Walk along the beach more.

Write more.

Connect more with others.

Laugh, laugh, did I say laugh?

Don't let an opportunity pass you by.

Do what fills you with positive energy.

I await your tapping.

Love, Dad

I CAN'T EXPLAIN WHY I was moved to tap to my dad. I can't explain why the questions and answers came so quickly. I only know there was an energy inside of me that moved me to actions. I don't really know if it was his spirit I was connecting to or merely my heart felt experiences of my dad that came through in these writings. I am not sure it matters. What matters, as always, is the effect of the answering of that call. What matters is that my loneliness was gone each time I tapped and my dad answered. What matters is I found out how important it is to live now and not in the past or future.

• • •

Epilogue

AFTER SEVERAL WEEKS of tapping to my father and his tapping
back, I stopped. I realized I was ready to do something about
those answers my father was giving me. It was right after that
mistake I made of typing to Dad on the wrong typewriter and
the ribbon getting all messed up and stuck.

I felt a need to find all the books on death and dying I had read
and saved on my book shelves. The same urge moved me to make
sure they were out of my house. I couldn't get them into my car
and to the used bookstore fast enough. Interesting.

But I knew I was finished reading about death and dying. I was
ready to play more, live life to its fullest, and let life unfold.
I was ready to surrender and accept what each day might offer.
I brought the Smith Corona Typewriter to the garage so I would
remember to get the ribbon fixed. I left the Royal out in my
special room to remind myself that I could connect with my
dad any time I wanted. His words would flow no matter what
typewriter I used.

It's been two months since I tapped. Since that time, I have
enrolled in a Qigong class, taken an art class, attended a concert
with friends, planned trips to Kauai and Sedona, created a needed seminar and focused on developing more joy in my life.

I wish to be more in a state of wonder instead of being concerned
with death.

· · ·

Gifts from my Dad

I am always with you, safe in your heart
I always believed in you
Family matters
Never be afraid to ask for what you need
Don't waste rubber bands
Women need more education to be equal in this life
Fight for what is important and then let it go
Celebrate each day you have to live another day
Thank those who give life
Either find sweetness each day or add it
Until you know, be open
Be generous
Find someone who provides space for you to be you
Keep your mind alert
Trust in your own journey
Play more
See your own country
Uphold your yes
Take responsibility
Do not be possessed by your possessions
Leaders see what is, listen and make things better
Everyone has a story: take time to listen before judging
When you have the ability to give, then give
No one can predict the end, so live each moment
DANCE MORE!

Acknowledgments

This small but meaningful book might not have been possible but for the generosity of Liz and John Vernon, the friends who happily gave me their typewriters to start the journey.

I am grateful to Tyler Callister, editor, who reviewed conversations and provided insightful feedback.

Thanks also to Jacqueline Gilman, who, in addition to designing this book, suggested that I include commentary that would allow the reader to have a deeper connection to my father and mother.

To my family and friends—Sue Davis, Agnes Liebhardt, Margaret Stewart, Lisa Pepper-Satkin and Gary Belford for sitting with the book and either reading or listening to the conversations and then inspiring me to publish them.

I must also include the film, *California Typewriter,* for arousing my curiosity and inspiring me to place my fingers on the keys of a typewriter once again.

To all, I am grateful.

CPSIA information can be obtained
at www.ICGtesting.com
Printed in the USA
FSHW021952021120
75518FS